Thrive! ... Affordably

THRIVE! ... AFFORDABLY

Your month-to-month guide to living your BEST life without breaking the bank.

Jennifer Streaks

Streaks Of Wisdom LLC
Washington, DC

Thrive! ... Affordably
Copyright © 2016 Jennifer Streaks
Streaks Of Wisdom LLC

ALL RIGHTS RESERVED.

No part of this book may be reproduced or transmitted in any form or by any means, electronic or mechanical, including photocopying, recording, or by any information storage or retrieval system, without permission in writing from the Publisher.

CONTENTS

Foreword	1
Introduction	5
Your Financial Wish List	6

January
January: Getting Started	13

February
February: Check Your Credit/Check Your Tax Deductions	19

March
March: The Tax Man Cometh	25

April
April: Getting Your House in Order	31

May
May: Accelerating Savings and Investing Goals	37

June
June: Develop a 3 Legged Stool of Income	43

July
July: Relax...A Little	49

August
August: Keep Learning	55

September
September: Refresh Your Goals	61

October
    October: Remain Focused   67

November
    November: Gearing Up For The Holidays   73

December
    December: Gauging Your Success   79

Your Finances
    Your Financial Accounts   85
    Your Financial Contact Info   86
    Quarterly Review Templates   87
    Spending Notes: Very Important!   92
    Your Personal Budget   94
    The Everyday Way to Save   95
    Lessons Learned   97
    Financial Goals: Let's Get a Jump on the New Year   99

Tips and Resources You Can Use
    Quick Tips for Everyday Living   103
    Financial News You Can Use!   108
    The End (?)   110
    Notes   115

Dedication   123

FOREWORD

Think to yourself. Why are you reading this book?

- Tired of working two jobs?
- Want more cash at the end of the month?
- Need to create residual income?
- Realizing you do not have job security?

Right now you are probably facing some financial challenges that you have finally decided to take control of. That is great, and this book will definitely help you do that. But I have to say that if you are not ready to be honest, then this book and any other book like it will not help you in your desire to be financially sound.

There are so many of us that do not understand how to handle money. We don't know what questions to ask or actions to take once financial troubles rear their ugly heads. Money is typically not discussed in households or taught in most schools (although it should be). So most people think that if they just make *more* money that their problems will be taken care of. That is not true. If you do not know how to handle your money, you will always have problems no matter how much money you acquire.

Understand that finally admitting that you are having problems is nothing to be ashamed of; rather, it is the smart, adult, mature thing to do. Committing to taking action to improve your financial situation and money management skills is the best thing you can do. It will allow you to sleep better, breathe easier, and have that peace of mind that money in the bank will give you.

This book is based on the months of the year because using the information in this book every month for a full year will create new saving and spending habits, new money management skills, and will leave you with a bank account(s) that ensures your financial security!

Take a moment and think about how you have been managing your money. How has it made you feel? Secure and responsible, or harried and worried? When unexpected expenses come up, are you prepared or are you taking from one bill to pay another? When travel opportunities arise, are you in a position to plan a great time or do you wait until the last minute because you have to see how your finances will be at that time?

A Bankrate.com survey found that 76% of Americans are living paycheck to paycheck. Is this you? Are you one unexpected expense away from financial ruin? And a FINRA Investor Education Foundation survey found that more and more Americans spend way more than they earn. From people making $40,000 to those making over $100,000, everyone overspends. So no, it is not about how much money you make, but how you manage it.

This book will help you with that. I wanted to put together a tool that will help you use your money wisely. I understand that we all want to live a good life. Travel, eat well, and live in a nice neighborhood. I get it. But you have to do it the right way.

As a Financial and Affordable Lifestyle Expert, I have developed financial and lifestyle tips to increase your financial knowledge, keep money in your pocket, manage debt and put you on the road to financial health and wellness.

That is the purpose of *THRIVE...AFFORDABLY!* I want you to not only *read* this book, but USE this book. Write in it, highlight in it. I have left pages for you to place pictures of wants and desires. You can think of this as your financial vision board. Write about your feelings about your money and where you want to be a year from now financially.

In a year, this book should be well-worn, written in, pages dog-eared, photos and post-it notes inside. This is your personal financial journey. That is why this book is "personal use size," because you can toss this book in your bag and take it with you wherever you go. Sit with friends and discuss chapters of the book, if you need an accountability partner, get one and work on the "to do" lists together.

This book will not only teach you how to save and spend, but also how to **plan** to spend! Planning to spend will make sure you do not *overspend.* Read this again: **If you plan to spend, you will not overspend.**

Understand that no one wants to just pay bills and die! This tool will help you live **your best life without breaking the bank!** Don't continue living paycheck to paycheck, being unprepared for unexpected expenses, or living on credit cards!

By taking this step, you have created the opportunity to change your life for the better and finally have the life you work for and deserve!

Don't just survive...THRIVE!!!

INTRODUCTION

Welcome to THRIVE!...*Affordably!* This book is designed to help you meet your financial goals for the year while pursuing the life you have always wanted to live! The Task? Getting organized, mastering basic financial management lessons, and breaking these tasks into smaller, more manageable steps. Let's get started!

I really want you to get personal, be honest, be open and be true about *YOUR* finances.

YOUR FINANCIAL WISH LIST

What does financial control mean to you? Does it mean paying your bills on time? Saving more out of each paycheck? The ability to travel? Being able to work part-time? Getting closer to retirement? Write your thoughts below and then find words and photos that underscore your thoughts for the Notes pages in the back.

_____

_____

_____

_____

What financial lessons have you already learned? Are you good at saving, paying bills, finding great deals? What financial decisions are you happiest with?

_____

_____

_____

_____

What about your financial missteps? Where would you like to see improvement? What kind of mistakes did you make last year? What scares you about taking control of your finances?

_____

_____

_____

_____

What are your long-term financial goals? Where do you see yourself with your finances in 5 to 10 years? Do you want to be a business owner, own your home, increase your savings, or be retired?

_____

_____

_____

_____

Your Financial Goals

By the end of the year, you would like to have achieved the following:

Earnings:

_____

_____

_____

_____

Savings:

_____

_____

_____

_____

Debt Elimination:

_____

_____

_____

_____

Other (philanthropic endeavors, retirement goals, better spending habits):

_____

_____

_____

_____

Money Tip

To make your financial goals less daunting, focus on how you will feel once you accomplish them and focus on the reason for your goals in the first place. Don't let the "how" get in the way.

JANUARY

A time of new beginnings

JANUARY: GETTING STARTED

Action Items

1.) **Find your finances.** Use the table at the end of this planner and make a complete list of your financial accounts, debts, assets and any other relevant information, together with contact information.

2.) **Clean House.** Get rid of unnecessary clutter that comes into your mailbox, inbox etc. Any magazines or catalogues that will tempt you to spend should be discarded.

3.) **Protect your identity.** Get rid of old credit card and bank account statements. Anything that has personal financial information on it should be shredded, not left where it can be easily found.

4.) **Use automated billing whenever possible.** This will help avoid the buildup of paperwork, make it less likely to miss a bill payment, and keep account numbers secure.

Your To Do List

1. _____

2. _____

3. _____

Money Tip

As you begin to work toward accomplishing your financial goals, you may want to consider a financial advisor. This is a good time of year to get on board with a financial advisor and/or tax preparer.

Goal:

Your financial goal for January is

_____.

Notes, Thoughts, Images:

FEBRUARY

Time to take stock

FEBRUARY: CHECK YOUR CREDIT/CHECK YOUR TAX DEDUCTIONS

Action Items

1.) **Get control of debt.** If you are carrying high levels of credit card debt, personal loans, or student loan debt, develop a plan for paying it off. Start by acknowledging the debt and listing your debt items.

2.) **You are entitled to a free credit report once a year.** Go to a website like freecreditreport.com. Review for any errors that may be impacting your credit score and contact the respective credit bureaus (Experian, Equifax or TransUnion) to fix any errors that you find.

3.) **Check your deductions on your W-4 tax form.** Many people get a large tax refund every year. This actually should not be the case. You are giving the federal government a tax free loan instead of you using that money throughout the year.

4.) **Make sure you have the right credit card for you.** Know what kind of credit card user you are. If you pay your credit cards off each month, then obtain a credit card with the best rewards or a cash back card. If you carry a balance from month to month, then find the lowest interest rate possible. Use credit card resources like creditcards.com to find the best card for you.

Your To Do List

1. _____

2. _____

3. _____

Money Tip

Don't just sit there and take what the credit card company offers you. If you are a good customer and pay on time, check and make sure your interest rate is reasonable. If it is on the high side, call your credit card company and ask them to adjust it for you. They want to keep your business, so they will usually work with you.

Goal:

Your financial goal for February is

_____.

Notes, Thoughts, Images:

MARCH

Make a list and check it twice

MARCH: THE TAX MAN COMETH

Action Items

1.) **Tax prep:** Are you ready to file your taxes next month? Review all anticipated deductions that might apply to you. To be sure, you might want to consider hiring a tax preparer.

2.) **Be sure that all healthcare, charitable donations, and business deductions are present and accounted for.** Get everything you are entitled to!

3.) **Perform a financial check in every quarter.** Using the checklist at the end of this planner, review all of your accounts (retirement, savings, investing, insurance) to see how well things are going and if any improvements need to be made.

Your To Do List

1. _____

2. _____

3. _____

Money Tip

Millions of taxpayers are audited every year through no fault of their own because they are selected randomly. Be sure to save all of your paperwork and receipts. If you use a tax preparer, part of their service should be that they will accompany you if you are called before the IRS to be audited.

Goal:

Your financial goal for March is

_____.

Notes, Thoughts, Images:

APRIL

Be Honest Here

APRIL: GETTING YOUR HOUSE IN ORDER

Action Items

1.) **Find out where your money is going.** Get a hold of your monthly bills, annual contributions or obligations, and daily expenses, if any. Gather credit statements, financial journals, and bank statements and upload into an excel spreadsheet or into Mint.com, which is a great personal finance tool. Now schedule any maintenance, repairs or health requirements in a manner that will save money. An ounce of prevention is worth a pound of cure!

2.) **Keep a financial journal.** Keep track of where your money goes every day. Keep all receipts and write down all spending for the next two weeks so you can see exactly what you spend your money on. Some expenses will shock you. Check for throwaway expenses: that 3 in the afternoon cup of coffee every day, meeting friends for drinks after work all the time, eating out three to four times a week.

3.) **Develop a personalized budget.** This is where you have to be honest about who you are. If the budget is too restrictive, you will break it; if it is too lax, then it won't do you any good. Look for areas where you can tighten your belt and eliminate waste. This is why it is called getting your house in order. As a start, use the Your Personal Budget page in the back of this planner.

Your To Do List

1. _____

2. _____

3. _____

Money Tip

Developing a budget does not have to be a daunting task, but it must be an honest one. Understand and be truthful with yourself about where you spend money needlessly. If you spend too much, this might be a time to ask yourself why. Also, incorporate the "why" and the "what" into your budget. Why are you saving and what are you saving for?

Goal:

Your financial goal for April is

_____.

Notes, Thoughts, Images:

MAY

What Is Your Plan?

MAY: ACCELERATING SAVINGS AND INVESTING GOALS

Action Items

1.) There was a State Farm study that concluded that fewer than half of American families have a financial back-up plan. Here is a financial test: Could you handle a financial emergency, such as a major home repair or job loss? Do you have an emergency/ rainy day fund with at least eight months to one year's worth of living expenses? This kind of financial back-up plan can go a long way toward you resting easier and will provide the necessary cash in an unexpected emergency. If you do not have an emergency fund, now is the time to start one.

2.) Think about your life and what you want out of it. Home ownership, the ability to travel, education, and retirement; there are numerous reasons to save. Even a little bit towards your goal will add up quickly. Work up to saving at least 15% of your income.

Your To Do List

1. _____

2. _____

3. _____

Money Tip

Financial issues have been the source of stress and health issues for decades. You are doing yourself a favor by saving and preparing for the future. It will bring you great peace of mind.

Goal:

Your financial goal for May is

_____.

Notes, Thoughts, Images:

JUNE

One is Not Enough

JUNE: DEVELOP A 3 LEGGED STOOL OF INCOME

Action Items

1.) **Take stock of your income at this point.** Are you reaching your highest potential? Have you ever thought of doing something different? Starting a business, writing a book? While everyone else is planning beach vacations, take this time to plan your future.

2.) **Invest in yourself and your goals.** This would be a good time to go back to school, hire a career coach, or take a few classes on entrepreneurship.

3.) **Go Big or Go Home.** Is it time to freelance in an area that you might consider pursuing full-time, ask for a raise or apply for a promotion? Give your earnings a boost.

4.) **Check in on yourself with a mid-year review.** At this time, the year is flying by. Where are you with your financial goals? Has it all been smooth sailing or have you encountered some bumps along the way? What improvements would you make and is there anything that you may have uncovered that you now want to work on?

Your To Do List

1. _____

2. _____

3. _____

Money Tip

The 3 legged stool of income is important because it keeps you financially secure. This means you have at least three streams of income coming in. Even if you are working full-time, it may be possible to do some freelance work on the side, write a book, edit manuscripts etc. Having multiple streams of income will allow you to save more money or have money on hand for expenses and emergencies.

Goal:

Your financial goal for June is

_____.

Notes, Thoughts, Images:

JULY

A Little Pat on the Back

JULY: RELAX...A LITTLE

Action Items

1.) Review your goals and to do lists and celebrate what you have accomplished thus far. Have you paid off a credit card, cleared up those errors on your credit report, or started a rainy day fund? Bask in this for a moment. Enjoy a movie, dinner, or a nice bottle of wine.

2.) **Get creative.** Replace after work happy hours and shoe shopping with free concerts in the park or cooking classes (you can make a great meal to take to work for lunch). Every city has websites that list fun activities found around that city.

Your To Do List

1. _____

2. _____

3. _____

Money Tip

Now that summer is here, set an activity budget. It is easy to get caught up in all of the events that will be taking place over the next few months, but make sure that you are clear about how much you want to spend and your financial goals.

Goal:

Your financial goal for July is _____.

Notes, Thoughts, Images:

AUGUST

Gear Up

AUGUST: KEEP LEARNING

Action Items

1.) **Read all about it.** Personal finance is not mastered overnight. Thinking about opening an investment account, IRA, or refinancing your home? Read up on it. There are many books, websites and blogs that cover such topics and provide you with great information. Feel free to ask questions and watch your knowledge grow!

2.) **Get ready for Fall.** This will be the time to bear down and finally get your list completed.

Your To Do List

1. _____

2. _____

3. _____

Money Tip

This tends to be a quiet month. Take this time to think about where you are. It is ok to be still and get ready.

Goal:

Your financial goal for August is

_____.

Notes, Thoughts, Images:

SEPTEMBER

Assess

SEPTEMBER: REFRESH YOUR GOALS

Action Items

1.) **Where are you in your financial goals now?** Checking, savings, retirement. All of these accounts should be well under way. Health insurance, car insurance, homeowners' insurance should all be in order as well.

2.) **Automatic deductions:** Since you have now gotten used to saving, this would be a good time to set up automatic savings withdrawals from your paycheck. This way you don't even have to think about it. Savings on automatic pilot!

3.) **Don't forget your quarterly review.** September is a good time to check in and see how you are progressing towards your financial goals. Make any improvements that may be necessary.

Your To Do List

1. _____

2. _____

3. _____

Money Tip

Now is a good time to review all home and car maintenance requirements. Make sure everything is ship-shape for the change in seasons. To be prepared is half the victory!

Goal:

Your financial goal for September is
_____.

Notes, Thoughts, Images:

OCTOBER

In the Zone

OCTOBER: REMAIN FOCUSED

Action Items

1.) **Become your very own Martha Stewart.** Home-cooked meals, at-home dinners with friends, and a nicely decorated home translate into more nights in instead of eating and having drinks out or ordering in. Design your environment to be what you want so that you are content at home and will save those dollars.

2.) **Money spent to enhance your life or make you more effective is money well spent.** Review your goals and make sure you have the resources necessary to accomplish them. If you have to invest in yourself to make it happen, do so.

Your To Do List

1. _____

2. _____

3. _____

Money Tip

If you will be traveling for the holidays, now is the time to start planning so that you can take advantage of travel deals (air fare, train, rental car, etc.).

Goal:

Your financial goal for October is
_____.

Notes, Thoughts, Images:

NOVEMBER

Stay Strong

NOVEMBER: GEARING UP FOR THE HOLIDAYS

Action Items

1.) **The holidays can be a budget buster if you are not careful.** Make travel plans as far in advance as possible to have time to search for deals and incentives. Use websites like hotwire.com or hotels.com so that you can compare prices and maybe get a great deal on a package travel plan. Be as flexible as possible on travel dates and times.

2.) **Don't fall into the gift trap.** The holidays are not about how much you spend on a gift, but quality time spent. Encourage family members to go in on gifts together, donate to charity, or have a homemade gift-making party.

3.) **Shop around.** Sales will be everywhere, so shopping around for the best deal on an item makes sense and can save a lot of money. Compare prices online and don't forget to shop the clearance and discount racks.

4.) **Leave the plastic at home.** Resist the urge to use your credit card for purchases. It is more difficult to keep track of what you spend and that line of credit will intensify your urge to buy. The worst part: You will still be paying interest on that purchase long after that present is unwrapped, used and pushed to the back of the closet.

5.) **Budget.** Many online sites offer tools such as spending worksheets and a calculator to estimate what you can afford to spend based on your income. Once you have determined that number, stick to it. Create a list of each person you need a gift for and include an amount to spend for them. Stick to that list and mark through each person as you finish shopping for them.

Your To Do List

1. _____

2. _____

3. _____

Money Tip

When it comes to holiday parties, don't try to do it all or pay for it all yourself. Plan potlucks and bybb's (bring your best bottle) for holiday gatherings. That way everyone can share in the cost.

Goal:

Your financial goal for November is

_____.

Notes, Thoughts, Images:

DECEMBER

Yes!!

DECEMBER: GAUGING YOUR SUCCESS

Action Items

1.) **Review your financial status.** Have you met your goals? What have you learned? What will you do differently in the New Year? Complete the Lessons Learned worksheet at the end of the planner.

2.) **Get a jump on the New Year.** Any new goals? Anything still left to do?

3.) **Complete your final review of the year!** Celebrate your accomplishments and make any adjustments needed as the year draws to a close.

Your To Do List

1. _____

2. _____

3. _____

Money Tip

Make a budget and stick to it for holiday gift giving. Don't rely on credit cards, use cash, shop around for sales and discounts and travel smart.

Goal:

Your financial goal for December is
_____.

Notes, Thoughts, Images:

YOUR FINANCES

YOUR FINANCIAL ACCOUNTS

	Account number	Lender/ Banker	Contributions	Code	Amount
Savings					
Earnings					
Retirement					
Insurance					
Assets					
Debt					

YOUR FINANCIAL CONTACT INFO

	Name:	Phone Number/Email
Financial Advisor:		
Checking/Savings:		
Mortgage Loan Info:		
Retirement:		
Insurance:		
Credit Card(s):		
Other:		

QUARTERLY REVIEW TEMPLATES

Quarterly Review Template: First Quarter Down: March

Under each item, write down changes, aspirations, challenges, and other comments.

Earnings:	Total:
Savings:	Total:
Investments:	Total:
Retirement:	Total:
Debt:	Total:

Mid-Year Review Template: Half-Way There! June

Under each item, write down changes, aspirations, challenges, and other comments.

Earnings:	Total:
Savings:	Total:
Investments:	Total:
Retirement:	Total:
Debt:	Total:

Quarterly Review Template: Third Quarter: September

Under each item, write down changes, aspirations, challenges, and other comments.

Earnings:	Total:
Savings:	Total:
Investments:	Total:
Retirement:	Total:
Debt:	Total:

Quarterly Review Template: Last One, How Did You Do?! December

Under each item, write down changes, aspirations, challenges, and other comments.

Earnings:	Total:
Savings:	Total:
Investments:	Total:
Retirement:	Total:
Debt:	Total:

SPENDING NOTES: VERY IMPORTANT!

Item	Why	Worth It	Amount

Spending Notes Continued:

Item	Why	Worth It	Amount

YOUR PERSONAL BUDGET

Think about what you want to spend your money on. What are your financial priorities? List the priorities from greatest to least.

Create four groupings:

Necessities (Housing, food, transportation)

Important Items (household and business expenses)

Savings

Entertainment and Luxuries

Now pull together your bank statements, credit card statements, and receipts as well as spending notes and see where your money is actually going. Ascertain the work you need to do to bring your reality closer to your personal budget created here.

THE EVERYDAY WAY TO SAVE

On this page, take a moment to think of ways and areas in which you can economize. Can you shop differently? Trim the cable bill? Enroll in your utility company's (gas, electric) budget plan?

Plan, Trim & Save!

LESSONS LEARNED

What did you accomplish this year? Did you meet all of your financial goals? What are you most proud of?

_____

_____

_____

_____

Where did you stumble? Are there things that you would change? Were there some hard choices you had to make?

_____

_____

_____

_____

Next year, what will you do differently? Have your financial goals changed? How do you view money and spending now?

_____

_____

_____

_____

FINANCIAL GOALS: LET'S GET A JUMP ON THE NEW YEAR

TIPS AND RESOURCES YOU CAN USE

QUICK TIPS FOR EVERYDAY LIVING

Happy Hour on a Budget

After a hard day's work we all want to unwind, but what is the best way to do that without breaking the bank?

- Take advantage of happy hour deals and drink specials like half price bottles of wine.
- Order small plates instead of an entrée and, most importantly, don't do happy hour every night.
- Happy hour at home is great, too. Invite a few friends over and have everyone bring a bottle of their favorite drink. It's much more cost effective and will control spending!

How Much to Tip in a Restaurant and When

When dining in a restaurant, what is the rule of thumb for tipping?

- Ordering drinks at the bar only? Tip a dollar per drink to the bartender.
- Ordering food at the bar? 10% of the bill.
- Dinner in the dining area with a waiter taking your order? 20% of the bill depending on service.

Getting through the Work Week without spending all of your cash

It is so easy Monday-Friday to spend all of your money on lunch, the 3pm snack or coffee break and happy hour. But if you continue to do this, you will always be broke.

- Starting now, bring lunch to work as often as you can stand it.
- Keep snacks in your desk for the 3pm slow down.
- Keep your brand of coffee at the office; all you have to do is add water.
- Decide now to do happy hour only a few times a month. Think of all of the money you will be saving as your motivation.

Traveling on a Budget

The best way to save money traveling is to plan ahead and leave early!

- Take advantage of online deals and package offers.
- Don't wait until the last minute to purchase tickets. The further ahead you purchase them, the cheaper the tickets will be.
- Instead of using a travel agent and having to pay their fee, use online travel sites like Expedia to get all your options laid out in one place. Also, if you can, get a package deal. Finding your airfare, hotel and car rental all in one will offer you the biggest savings.

The 5 Best Bargains for the Fall

Take time now to be ready to take advantage of these discounts in the Fall.

- The fall is a great time to shop for appliances because the upcoming new models are headed to the store and they want to get rid of the current year's models. There will be great sales in washer/dryers, refrigerators and other major appliances.
- November is a great time to shop for televisions and electronic gadgets. Stores will have deep discounts on these items because these are popular gifts during the holiday season.
- Grocery stores start their stock up sales right about this time. Look out for these circulars and coupons to stock up on canned goods and household essentials you will need heading into winter.

Back to School Savings

Most parents will spend over $500.00 per kid to get ready for the school year, here is how to reduce that amount:

- Take stock of last year's purchases. Odds are a lot of that stuff is still usable from rulers and pencils to notebook paper and backpacks. Don't buy anything until you go through last year's leftover supplies.
- Prepare an inventory list per child of what is needed from the class list of required supplies, not your child's list of wants.

- Look at past spending as a good indicator of what will be necessary for the upcoming year and to see where you can find bargains.
- When you head out to the store, carry cash. This is a good rule of thumb because when the cash is gone, the shopping is over. Also, prepare for a school shopping trip after the year starts. There will always be a few items that pop up after classes have started, which is why you don't want to blow your budget beforehand.

Thinking about starting a business? Here's how:

Right now, there is an explosion of entrepreneurs that will only continue to grow. There are many that have turned a side job into a main job or just decided to make a go of starting a new business.

- This is a great time to start a new venture, form your LLC, put together a website, order business cards, and establish social media accounts to get you up and running.
- A great business is typically based on an idea that solves a problem or gives a customer a unique experience. Once you have that, make sure that you market it so that potential customers know what you can do. Take advantage of all social media and the humble brag!
- Be sure that all appropriate and necessary business paperwork is filed and that your taxes are paid! Your business will be thriving in no time!

What to do when you want to buy a Home:

It has become tougher to buy a home. Many are now wondering what is the best way to get it right.

- First, before you do anything, get a copy of your credit report. Know where you stand with your credit before you go house hunting.
- How much of a down payment can you afford and how much house can you afford? You will typically be approved for three times your income, depending on your credit.
- Remember this: You do not have to buy at the top of what you are approved for.
- Put down as large of a down payment as possible so your monthly payment will be less.

FINANCIAL NEWS YOU CAN USE!

Websites

Creditcards.com (find the best credit card for you)

Dailyworth.com (personal finance articles

Napfa.org (find a fee-only financial advisor)

Bankrate.com (free calculators, mortgage, debt, retirement etc.)

JenniferStreaks.com (always check in here for financial news updates)

Books

Rich Dad Poor Dad by Robert Kiyosaki and Sharon L. Lechter

Secrets of the Millionaire Mind by T. Harv Eker

One Small Step Can Change Your Life by Robert Maurer

Magazines

MONEY Magazine

Kiplinger's Personal Finance Magazine

Smart Money Magazine

THE END (?)

Don't you for one minute think that your purpose is just to pay bills and die! You are meant to THRIVE! Taking control of your finances is one of the most important things you can do to live a better life, a good life.

Don't think that you are not smart enough or that you don't already have enough money to live a comfortable life. It only takes small changes done consistently to get you to your goal.

Will it get hard? Yes! There are so many things that we all want for ourselves and our families, but know that you may not be able to do it all at one time, but that does not mean never. It means PLAN!

Yes, so many make financial mistakes due to a lack of planning and a lack of awareness.

So what does planning entail?

1.) **Take control of your credit!** I cannot say this enough. Think of your credit as the foundation for your financial house. Without good credit, you won't be able to do the things you want to financially. Once you get your credit on track, protect it. Get a copy of your credit report twice a year, don't apply for credit unless you sure to want to buy (this can lead to unwanted inquiries on your report), and do not co-sign a loan of any kind for anyone!

2.) **Get an emergency fund together.** Before you do any other kind of investing, make sure you have eight months or more of expenses saved and put away and don't touch it, unless it is a real emergency (job loss, long-term illness).

3.) **Make sure you are covered.** You should have health insurance, car insurance, homeowners insurance, and renters insurance at the right levels to insure that if you have an accident, you are covered and you won't have to go through savings or all of your cash to make things right.

4.) **Travel. Always plan ahead!** You will get the best deals if you are flexible with times and dates. Planning ahead will give you the time you need to research prices on airfare, hotel, and rental car options. When you travel last minute or are in a rush, you end up paying so much more.

5.) **Multiple streams of income.** Get a part-time job, offer up your services, become a virtual assistant, blogger, social media poster, proofreader, etc. Get the idea? Find ways to bring in more money, even if your primary position covers everything; you can always save the extra money. And you never what might happen: if you get laid off, downsized or hours cut, you won't go into panic because you have other money coming in.

6.) **Life Insurance.** You may not think about this, but this is important. If something were to happen to you, who would take care of your funeral expenses or your home or condo if you own one? The leading cause of death for those under 45 comes from accidents, especially car accidents. It may seem morbid

to think about, but you don't want your parents to have to deal with the loss of a son or daughter – and incur a financial expense on top of that.

7.) **Taxes.** The dreaded "T"! As your financial picture grows, taxes become a big part of it. It is very easy to end up owing Uncle Sam if you are not paying attention to how much taxes are being withheld from your paycheck. As your salary increases, it would be wise to engage a tax preparer to get you on the right track and make sure that you are giving Uncle Sam his due. If you do find yourself owing taxes, make payment arrangements immediately! Don't let this fester. For as long as the bill is unpaid, interest and penalty accrues and increases the total amount you owe. If you don't take this seriously, and the IRS has to come after you for unpaid taxes, it could result in a tax lien. You do not want that.

8.) **Keeping Up Appearances.** Don't! Anyone having financial problems should have an honest conversation with friends and family. Typically, if you are trying to brush it under the rug, you are also not being honest with yourself and this will only lead to your financial problems getting worse. It is better to be upfront and state that you are having financial problems and that you are in the process of working them out. Also, state that since you are working out financial issues, you will be cutting back, not taking that expensive family vacation or eating out every week. Having the conversation also shows that you are taking responsibility and are serious about changing your situation.

9.) **Recognize when you need a financial diet.** It is so easy to get used to a certain lifestyle, expensive car or apartment, extravagant dinners and high-end wardrobes. But what happens when you need to save money for something or if you need to make a change? It could be a decision to purchase a home, go back to school or to get your financial house in order. You may have to decrease your spending now to achieve a much larger goal later. Take a look at your financial lifestyle. Do you have the expensive car, but don't own your home? Do you run out of money before your next paycheck? Are you lacking an emergency fund? Now is the time to go on a financial diet for your greater good. Maybe get a smaller apartment, when the car lease is up get a less expensive car, do a little less clothes shopping and put that money to better use like buying a condo or beefing up your savings. Don't look at it as a negative. Look at it as sacrificing now so you can enjoy even more down the road. So you can Thrive!

10.) **The Will.** Yes, you need a will. As soon as you start amassing assets: Purchase a home, start building up that IRA or 401k, start investing in stocks or mutual funds or start a business, you will need a will to lay out how you want everything handled, and who gets what in the event of your death.

Understand that respecting your money is respecting yourself!

1.) **Don't spend money on unnecessary things.** Think before you spend. Is that purchase a need or a want? And, if it is a want, can you really afford it right now?

2.) **Understand where your money is going and why.** I hear people say all the time, by the end of the week, the end of the month or a week before payday, they are broke and can't figure out why. Know where your money is going and create a budget so your money goes further and lasts longer.

3.) **Save, save, save!!** I say this all the time, but there are so many people living from paycheck to paycheck. This is no way to live. Not setting aside money for a rainy day leaves you financially vulnerable and emotionally stressed out.

Always remember, respecting your money is respecting yourself. If you can get control of your money and understand how important it is to have a long term view of your finances that will be money in the bank!

Thank you for allowing me on the start of your journey! Now it is time to take all you have learned and THRIVE!

NOTES

NOTES

NOTES

NOTES

NOTES

NOTES

NOTES

DEDICATION

This book is dedicated to my family and friends, those who have supported me through it all! Also, to those striving to live their best life, it is never about the fall or even the struggle, but the get up and the triumph!

We all have an opportunity to THRIVE!!

www.ingramcontent.com/pod-product-compliance
Lightning Source LLC
Chambersburg PA
CBHW070527010526
44110CB00050B/2198